LANGUAGE ARTS EXPLORER

THE LIFE CYCLES OF PLANTS

by Rebecca Hirsch

SCIENCE LAB:
THE LIFE CYCLES OF PLANTS

CHERRY LAKE PUBLISHING • ANN ARBOR, MICHIGAN

CHERRY
LAKE
Publishing

Published in the United States of America
by Cherry Lake Publishing
Ann Arbor, Michigan
www.cherrylakepublishing.com

Printed in the United States of America
Corporate Graphics Inc
September 2011
CLFA09

Consultants: Karen O'Connor, co-owner, Mother Earth Gardens, Minneapolis, Minnesota; Gail Saunders-Smith, associate professor of literacy, Beeghly College of Education, Youngstown State University

Editorial direction: Design and production:
Lisa Owings   Craig Hinton

Photo credits: Dave Hughes/iStockphoto, cover, 1; Shutterstock Images, 5, 7, 15, 20; Dmitri Sevcenko/Fotolia, 8; Steve Shoup/Bigstock, 11; S.J. Krasemann/Photolibrary, 12; Chad Zuber/Shutterstock Images, 16; Dreamstime, 18; Clay Perry/Photolibrary, 19; Andrew F. Kazmierski/Shutterstock Images, 22; Fabio Fersa/Shutterstock Images, 23; Gladskikh Tatiana/Shutterstock Images, 27

Library of Congress Cataloging-in-Publication Data
Hirsch, Rebecca E.
  Science lab. The life cycles of plants / by Rebecca Hirsch.
    p. cm. – (Language arts explorer. Science lab)
  ISBN 978-1-61080-204-8 – ISBN 978-1-61080-293-2 (pbk.)
  1. Plants–Juvenile literature. 2. Plant life cycles–Juvenile literature. I. Title. II. Title: Life cycles of plants. III. Series: Language arts explorer. Science lab.

QK49.H57 2011
580–dc22
                         January 2013
                         2011015129

Cherry Lake Publishing would like to acknowledge the work of The Partnership for 21st Century Skills. Please visit www.21stCenturySkills.org for more information.

TABLE OF CONTENTS

You are being given a mission. The facts in What You Know will help you accomplish it. Remember the clues from What You Know while you are reading the story. The clues and the story will help you answer the questions at the end of the book. Have fun on this adventure!

All plants, from the tiniest weeds to the tallest trees, go through similar stages of life. They move through these stages in some of the hottest, coldest, driest, and wettest places on Earth. Your mission is to find out how scientists study the **life cycles** of plants. What kinds of experiments help them understand how plants survive in tough places? What kinds of questions do they ask? Read the facts in What You Know, and then start your mission to discover the lives of plants.

WHAT YOU KNOW

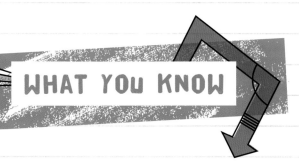

★ Every green plant needs the same things to survive: sunlight, air, water, and room to grow.

★ The parts of a plant work together. Roots soak up water. Leaves make food from sunlight. The stem carries food and water to the rest of the plant.

★ Many plants make flowers. The purpose of a flower is to make seeds. Seeds are the **offspring** of plants.

Water lilies make their way through mud and water before blooming above the surface.

★ Mushrooms are a type of fungus. Both mushrooms and plants grow in the ground, but they are different. Plants make their own food from sunlight. Mushrooms do not.

Ryo Tanabe is a reporter from *Green Kids* magazine. He has been sent to interview experts and investigate the life cycles of plants. Carry out your mission by reading his journal.

A plant begins life as a seed. At first, the seed is **dormant**, or asleep. The seed awakens only when the conditions are just right—the right amount of warmth and moisture. Some seeds need sunlight, and others need a cold spell. Then the seed starts to grow.

When a seed starts to grow, we say it **germinates**. First, the seed soaks up water. Then the **seed coat**, a protective shell around the seed, cracks open. A tiny root pokes out and pushes downward through the soil. A tiny shoot pokes out and grows upward through the soil. The shoot breaks through the soil to the sunlight, and the first leaves open. This tiny plant is called a **seedling**.

These are the first few stages of a plant's life cycle. I am here at Borealis Nursery in Wisconsin to learn more. Michelle Velasquez works at Borealis, where plants are grown to sell in stores. She is showing me around.

She opens the door to a greenhouse, and we walk inside. Even though it is cool outside, it feels warm and tropical inside. We walk down the center aisle, looking at the plants, which are growing in pots on tables.

Ms. Velasquez shows me pots with tiny plants poking out of the soil. They are snapdragon seedlings. Nearby,

Snapdragon flowers stay closed until a bee comes to open them.

some bigger snapdragons are growing. They are bushy and have pink flowers.

Here is what I learn about how snapdragons grow: After the seed germinates, the seedling grows and grows. It gets taller and sprouts more leaves. Soon it is ready to make flowers. Flowers allow plants to reproduce, or make offspring. The offspring are the seeds.

"With seeds, the whole life cycle starts again," Ms. Velasquez says. "It begins with a seed and ends with more seeds."

Pollen sticks to hairs on the bodies and legs of bees.

Ms. Velasquez tells me she is testing how different growing conditions affect the snapdragon's life cycle. Here is how her experiments work: All the plants are grown in the same soil, with the same light, and at the same temperature. Then she changes just one thing. This month, she has given one set of plants more water than the others. Every week she measures how tall the plants are and counts how many flowers they have. If she sees a difference, she knows it is because those plants received different amounts of water. This way, she can find the best way to grow snapdragons for the nursery.

POLLINATION

Flowers make pollen. Before a seed can grow, the powdery pollen must be spread to a part of the flower called the stigma. Snapdragons rely on bees to pollinate them. Before a bee lands, the flower is closed, and a flap of petal covers the opening. The bee, covered in pollen from other flowers, lands on a petal that looks like a landing pad. If the bee is the right size and weight, the flap pops open. The bee crawls inside. As it searches for nectar to eat, the bee brushes against the stigma, pollinating the flower. Other flowers rely on moths, birds, or bats to pollinate them. Some flowers spread their pollen on the wind.

After I wave good-bye, I'm filled with questions. Life seems easy for a plant in a greenhouse. The temperature is always perfect. There is always plenty of light and water. But most plants don't live in a greenhouse. Most plants don't have a person to take care of them. How do plants live out their lives in more difficult places? ★

I've arrived at my next stop—the Saguaro Botanical Garden near Phoenix, Arizona. Sweat is running down my face. I spot a thermometer on the wall. It reads 103 degrees Fahrenheit (40°C).

There is water here in the desert, just not much. Rainfall is light, and it doesn't come often. The sun is hot, so the ground dries quickly after a rain.

Tony Castillo is showing me around the garden. He is showing me the plants that grow here. I'm surprised. I thought only cacti grew in the desert. But trees and flowers grow here too.

I ask how these plants survive in such a hot, dry place. Mr. Castillo tells me that long roots are one way. Mesquite trees have roots that go deep into the earth in search of water. Other plants have roots that run outward just under the surface. These plants can soak up water from a wide circle of ground. Cacti absorb water quickly and store it inside them. They have a thick, waxy skin to keep the water from escaping. The needles keep animals away and shade the skin from the scorching sun.

Mr. Castillo's job at the botanical garden is to research wildflowers that grow in the desert. We are now in

Many cacti produce flowers. The blooms only last for a few days.

Mr. Castillo's office. It is cooler here, away from the hot sun. He shows me photographs of the desert on his computer. In photo after photo, the desert is covered with flowers—yellow, orange, purple, and pink flowers.

I'm amazed at what I see. Surely this can't be the same desert. I didn't see any of those bright-colored flowers growing outside. I ask whether those photos were shot in a different desert.

He tells me the photos were taken close by, just outside the botanical garden. The only difference is that these pictures were taken after a rain.

"The plants I study," he says, pointing to some orange-flowered plants in one of the photos, "survive by changing

Each spring, the Arizona desert sand becomes a carpet of blooms.

their life cycle to suit their environment. You won't see them growing here very often."

I learn that most of the time, the seeds are sleeping in the ground, waiting for rain. "Being asleep helps seeds survive in the desert," Mr. Castillo says. "Some might stay dormant for ten years. They must wait until they have enough water to grow."

When rain finally soaks the ground, the seeds leap into action. They germinate quickly, and the plants shoot up, rushing through their life cycle. Then the flowers bloom, and the whole desert explodes with color. If the plants grew more slowly, they would run out of water. Just before the plants die, they drop new seeds all over the desert. The whole cycle lasts just a few weeks. It is a life cycle that is suited to the desert.

I ask Mr. Castillo what sorts of experiments he does with these plants. He explains that he wondered how these plants scattered their seeds all over the desert. He is experimenting to learn how ants may help spread the seeds.

Desert ants live in colonies under the ground. Worker ants wander outside their colony, collecting seeds to eat. They fetch wildflower seeds and carry them back to the colony. But the ants drop some of the seeds along the way.

Mr. Castillo suspects the forgotten seeds may grow into new plants. He is testing his ideas. He observes some plants in a spot where there are no ants living nearby. He compares those plants with ones that grow near ant colonies. After a few years, he counts the number of plants and can learn which plants have reproduced better. ★

EVAPORATION IN THE DESERT

Desert plants hang onto every drop of water. Evaporation—water escaping into the air—can mean death. Wide, flat leaves lose a lot of water. Their large surfaces are exposed to the dry desert air. That is why desert plants have few leaves, small leaves, or no leaves at all.

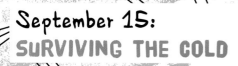
I have traveled to a vast forest in Alberta, Canada. The forest stretches all the way across Canada, Alaska, Russia, and Europe. Most of the trees here are **evergreens**. Their leaves are shaped like needles and stay green all year long.

Dr. Michael McCray is with me. He is a botanist who studies ferns that grow in the forest. He has agreed to show me around.

I ask Dr. McCray about ferns. He tells me they are an ancient type of plant. They were here when dinosaurs walked the earth. Ferns have roots and stems and leaves like most plants. But there is a big difference. Ferns don't make seeds. Instead, they make **spores**.

LIFE WITHOUT SEEDS

Ferns aren't the only plants that reproduce by spores. Mosses, club mosses, and horsetails also make spores. All of them are ancient plants. They have lived on Earth for hundreds of millions of years. Mushrooms reproduce by spores, too, but they aren't plants. Mushrooms are fungi, an entirely different kind of living thing.

Ferns reproduce using spores instead of seeds.

Dr. McCray squats down and shows me a fern leaf. On the underside are rows of small brown bumps. These bumps are where the spores are made. Ferns release their spores into the wind. This is how they reproduce.

"I study how spores grow into new plants," Dr. McCray says. "I grow ferns from spores and carefully observe every step of their growth. I have to use a microscope because spores are so small. Then I photograph what I see."

Dr. McCray explains that spores are simpler than seeds. Spores do not have the protective coats that seeds have. They need moisture to germinate and can only survive in damp places. I think of the evergreen trees that grow here. I wonder: how do they reproduce? Do they make spores or seeds?

Evergreen trees have many ways to survive cold weather.

Dr. McCray smiles and picks up a pinecone. "Evergreen trees make seeds. Each scale on the pinecone is a seed."

The wind is blowing. I zip up my jacket and shove my hands in my pockets. I ask him about the challenges of getting through the winter.

He tells me that in winter, getting enough water is a big challenge for plants. Soon the land will be covered with snow and ice. Everything will stay frozen for months. Trees can't soak up frozen water. To survive the winter, they must conserve water.

Evergreen tree needles have small surfaces, so less water evaporates. The needles also have a waxy coating to keep water from escaping. These are some of the ways the trees can survive the winter. ★

I have arrived in Costa Rica. I am standing in the rain forest in Corcovado National Park.

I have read a lot about tropical rain forests. I know they are warm, and they receive a lot of rain. I also know that plants thrive in this warm, moist environment. Rain forests have more plants than any other environment on Earth. Half of all the plant and animal species on Earth live in rain forests.

Dr. Maria Hughes is with me. She tells me that at least 150 inches (381 cm) of rain fall in this forest every

RAIN FOREST DESTRUCTION

Rain forests can be found all around the world. They grow in a belt that stretches along the equator. You can find rain forests in Asia, Australia, New Zealand, the Americas, and Africa. Unfortunately, people are cutting down and burning the rain forests. They use the land for farming and raising cattle. When rain forests disappear, rain forest animals disappear too. More species live in rain forests than anywhere else. That means rain forests are essential not only to the animals and people that live there, but to everyone on Earth.

In the rain forest, light must travel through many layers of plants to reach the ground.

year. I do a quick calculation in my notebook. That's more than 13 feet (4 m) of water!

Dr. Hughes works in the forest, searching for new rain forest plants. She is hoping to find some that can be used for medicine. She tells me that even though plants grow well here, life can be hard in a tropical rain forest.

One challenge is dealing with all that water. "See how the water makes beads on this leaf?" Dr. Hughes shows me a big heart-shaped leaf covered with droplets of water. "Those beads mean the leaf has a waxy coating. The wax keeps water out of the leaf. It's as if the leaf is wearing a raincoat."

Another big challenge is shade. The plants here grow so thick and tangled that almost no light reaches the ground through the layers of the rain forest.

Plants must compete with each other to get enough light. Trees do this by growing tall and fast. They race each other to be the first to spread their leaves in the sun. Vines have a sneakier way of getting into the light. They can't grow tall by themselves, but they can climb other plants.

Many plants don't even bother to grow on the dark ground. Instead, they grow on the limbs of trees. Their roots suck moisture right out of the air.

Orchids grow this way. Many orchid plants produce beautiful blooms. They spread seeds that are like dust. The seeds float through the jungle air. Some will land on a tree limb and start to grow. ★

Orchids don't need dirt to grow. Their roots absorb water from the air.

I have traveled to Lost Oak Forest in West Virginia. I am standing under some big oak trees. The acorns crunch under my feet as I walk. An acorn is an oak tree seed.

Mr. John Patterson is with me. He lives nearby and owns these woods. When Mr. Patterson bought this land, there were no trees here. The forest had been cut down for timber. He wanted to let it regrow. He started by planting small trees. Now the trees tower over our heads.

I remember what I learned in the rain forest, about plants not growing well in shade. I ask him about the acorns lying on the ground under the mother tree. Can they grow and survive here?

Squirrels help to spread the seeds of oak trees.

HOW SEEDS TRAVEL

Most seeds don't fall straight to the ground. Plants have ways to send their seeds out into the world. Dandelion seeds sail away on parachutes. Coconuts can float away on water. And many plants, such as oak trees, rely on animals to carry their seeds away.

Mr. Patterson tells me the acorns won't stay here. Someone else in the forest will take them and plant them. I wonder who he means.

Then I see them: squirrels. Two come racing past me. They chitter and chase each other up a tree. I can see their nest of dried leaves tucked high among the branches.

Mr. Patterson tells me squirrels love to eat acorns. Every fall squirrels race around, scooping acorns off the ground and burying them in a safe place. In winter they return, sniffing for acorns and digging them up for a meal. A squirrel can smell an acorn through a foot (.3 m) of snow!

Squirrel noses may be powerful, but they aren't perfect. Sometimes they miss an acorn. In spring, the forgotten acorn will start to grow. If it is buried in a good spot with plenty of sunshine, water, and room to grow, the acorn may someday grow into a full-sized oak tree.

Mr. Patterson says many plants and animals in the forest work together, helping each other. Just as he has

New life flourishes within fallen logs.

helped the oak trees by planting them, squirrels help too.
They help the tree complete its life cycle by spreading its
seeds. In return, the oak trees help the squirrels survive
the winter.

As I'm thinking about life cycles, I wonder how it all
ends. When is a plant's life cycle over?

Mr. Patterson shows me a fallen tree nearby. The tree
may be dead, but as I move closer, I can see signs of life.
Mushrooms are growing on it. They have an important job
to do. Mushrooms break down dead plants for food. So do
earthworms, beetles, and **bacteria**. They all work together
to recycle dead leaves and fallen logs in a process called
decomposition. Soon this log will be gone. In its place will
be a mound of dark, rich soil. At the end of its life, the plant
returns to the ground, releasing its nutrients into the soil.
A new plant will grow in its place. ★

For my last stop, I have traveled to Rockford, Illinois. I am standing in a farm field. All around me are rows and rows of plants. I'm here to learn about plants that people grow.

John Berksen has brought me to this field. He is a plant breeder, a scientist who breeds new varieties of plants. In one hand, he holds a big green cabbage. In the other, he holds a head of broccoli.

"Few people know," he says as he shows me the cabbage and broccoli, "that these are the same species,

Cabbage and broccoli were developed from the same wildflower.

the same kind of plant. They both are the offspring of a wildflower that grew in Europe."

I look at the two vegetables. How did that happen?

Thousands of years ago, a wildflower grew in Europe. Each wildflower plant was a little different from every other one. For instance, some had smaller leaves and some had bigger leaves. Leaf size is a trait that is inherited.

Long ago, people liked to eat the leaves of this wildflower. Every year, they planted the wildflower in their gardens. But they only collected seeds from the plants with the biggest leaves. The new plants inherited big leaves from their parents. Over the years, the plants that grew had bigger and bigger leaves. After hundreds of years, cabbage had been developed.

Some time after that, people realized the flower buds of this same wildflower tasted good too. Every year, they planted seeds from the plants with the most flower buds. Hundreds of years passed and, thanks to this selection process, broccoli was born.

Mr. Berksen tells me people have been changing plants for thousands of years. Plant breeders still do this. A plant breeder might try to develop a tomato that tastes better or a peach that can grow well in the cold or a rose with pink-speckled flowers.

Mr. Berksen is developing new kinds of cabbage. He wants to create cabbages that grow bigger, faster. If he makes a big cabbage that also tastes good, people may decide to buy it to grow in their farms and gardens.

People can change all kinds of plants, but plants also change on their own. Who knows what new plants will develop in the future? ★

Congratulations! You have learned a lot about the life cycles of plants. You've learned that all plants go through certain stages. A seed germinates, becomes a seedling, and then grows into a plant. The plant makes flowers, which make the seeds. Then the cycle begins again. You have discovered that some plants don't make flowers and seeds; they make spores instead. You have learned that plants grow in difficult places. They have life cycles that are suited to the conditions where they live. You have also learned that people can change plants for their own use. Congratulations on a mission well done!

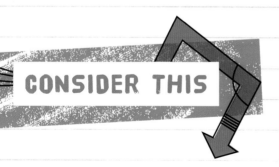

CONSIDER THIS

★ What happens when a seed germinates?

★ Cacti, rain forest leaves, and evergreen needles all have waxy coatings. Compare how the waxy coating is used by each plant. What is similar? What's different?

- ★ Cacti and evergreen trees both grow in challenging conditions. What is one thing that is different about these conditions? What is one thing that is similar?
- ★ In the book are examples of animals helping plants. Think of some other examples of an animal helping a plant complete its life cycle.
- ★ What is one way that plants have been changed by people?

One of the best ways to learn about plants is to carefully observe them.

GLOSSARY

bacteria (bak-TEER-ee-uh) single-celled organisms that can be seen only with a microscope

dormant (DOR-muhnt) asleep and not yet growing

evergreen (EV-ur-green) a plant that keeps its leaves in winter

germinate (JUR-muh-nate) when a seed begins to grow into a seedling

life cycle (LIFE sye-kuhl) the series of stages that a living thing passes through, from birth to death

offspring (AWF-spring) the young of plants or animals

pollen (PAH-luhn) a powdery dust that must be spread on the stigma before a flower can make seeds

seed coat (SEED koht) a protective shell around the seed

seedling (SEED-ling) a young plant grown from a seed; it has a root, a stem, and one or two leaves

spore (SPOR) a dust-like particle that can grow into a new plant

stigma (STIG-ma) the part of a flower that receives pollen

trait (TRAYT) a feature that is inherited, such as the size of a leaf or the color of a flower

LEARN MORE

BOOKS

Benbow, Ann, and Colin Mably. *Nature's Secret Habitats.* Berkeley Heights, NJ: Enslow Elementary, 2010.

Day, Jeff. *Don't Touch That! The Book of Gross, Poisonous, and Downright Icky Plants and Critters.* Chicago: Chicago Review Press, 2008.

Guiberson, Brenda Z. *Life in the Boreal Forest.* New York: Henry Holt and Company, 2009.

Hurtig, Jennifer. *Deciduous Forests.* New York: Weigl Publishers, 2007.

WEB SITES

The Great Plant Escape

http://urbanext.illinois.edu/gpe/gpe.html

Help solve the mysteries of how plants grow.

Plants-In-Motion

http://plantsinmotion.bio.indiana.edu/plantmotion/starthere.html

Watch movies showing how plants grow and move.

Rain Forest Alliance Kids' Corner

http://www.rainforest-alliance.org/kids

Play games and learn all about rain forest life.

SLEEPY SEEDS

What happens when seeds wake up? Choose some large seeds and investigate. Peas, beans, corn, sunflower seeds, or pumpkin seeds work well. Divide the seeds into two groups. Soak one set of seeds in a glass of water overnight. Then use a magnifying glass to examine and compare the groups of seeds. What do you notice about their size? What has happened to the seed coats? To continue watching the seeds germinate, slip them inside a jar or a plastic bag. Add a damp paper towel, and seal the jar or bag to keep moisture in. Watch the seeds for a few days. What happens?

TAKE A MINI-SAFARI

You don't have to travel the world to investigate plants. Just grab a notebook and a magnifying glass and head outside. Find some woods, your backyard, or a weedy lot to explore. Choose a one-foot by one-foot (.3 m by .3 m) square of land. Now investigate. How many different kinds of plants do you see? Find plants with smooth leaves, jagged leaves, big leaves, and tiny leaves. If you find flowers, look closely for developing seeds. Use your notebook to draw or write about what you see.

INDEX

Rebecca Hirsch holds a PhD in molecular biology from the University of Wisconsin–Madison. She worked as a plant biologist before becoming a writer. She writes for children and young adults on topics ranging from plants to polar bears. She lives with her husband and daughters in State College, Pennsylvania.

ABOUT THE CONSULTANTS

Karen O'Connor is co-owner of Mother Earth Gardens in Minneapolis, Minnesota, an independent garden center focusing on organic and sustainable gardening. She lives with her husband, two sons, and several small pets.

Gail Saunders-Smith is a former classroom teacher and Reading Recovery teacher leader. Currently she teaches literacy courses at Youngstown State University in Ohio. Gail is the author of many books for children and three professional books for teachers.